Early Health & Medicine

Bobbie Kalman

The Early Settler Life Series

Crabtree Publishing Company

In memory of my grandparents

*A special thanks to the following people without
whose help this book would not have been possible:*

Senior editor: *Lise Gunby*
Researcher and editor: *Maria Protz*
Assistant editors: *Susan Hughes*
                          Mary Ann Horgan
Freelance editor: *Dan Liebman*
Design and mechanicals: *Diane Taylor*
                                Nancy Cook
Photographers: *Sarah Peters*
                      Donna Acheson
Artwork pages 46 and 47: *Gary Pearson*
Picture researcher: *Noel Rutland*

*A thank you to Dr. Ernst W. Stieb
for his advice and encouragement*

Cataloging in Publication Data

*Kalman, Bobbie, 1947 -
    Early Settler Health and Medicine*

*(Early settler life series)
Includes index.*
ISBN   0-86505-031-7 *hardcover*
ISBN   0-86505-030-9 *softcover*

*1. Health - History. 2. Medical care - History.
I. Title.   II. Series.*

R149.K34 1983   613'.09'03   LC93-30698

350 Fifth Ave, Suite 3308
New York, NY 10118

R.R. #4
360 York Road
Niagara-on-the-Lake, ON
Canada L0S 1J0

73 Lime Walk
Headington, Oxford 0X3 7AD
United Kingdom

Contents

The doctor looks at his medical book to find a cure for this man's illness. The man complains of a sore throat and fever. The doctor does not know why his patient is ill. The sick man should be careful. The remedy the doctor prescribes could make him even sicker.

Health was a challenge

Today we take our health for granted. We have good food to eat, vitamins to take, and doctors who can cure us if we get sick. In the days of the early settlers, getting sick was more frightening than facing a pack of wolves in the dark. Any illness, no matter how small, could become serious enough that the patient could die. If serious illnesses did not cause death, some of the popular settler remedies might!

The mystery of the germ

People, including doctors, knew little about the causes of disease. Today we find certain diseases, such as cancer, very frightening because we do not know what causes them. The settlers did not know about germs. Without this knowledge, medicine was often guesswork. People had no idea why they became sick.

Today we know that many diseases are spread because one person catches germs from another. In the old days the settlers drank from unwashed cups which had been used by others. When they traveled they slept on dirty sheets where many others had slept. They did not wash themselves or their clothes very often. Settlers had no idea that cleanliness played a big part in good health. They did not know that germs thrive in unclean places.

The settlers did not know that sharing cups with others also meant sharing germs. These boys might come down with measles or chicken pox, when all they wanted was water!

Mother Nature to the rescue

It was surprising that the settlers survived at all with so many strikes against their health. However, Mother Nature was on their side. In those days, the air was fresher, and the sun shone more brightly. There was no smog. The settlers had to walk long distances and do hard physical work which kept their bodies in good shape. Their food contained no chemical preservatives. The trees, roots, and plants on the homestead provided the settlers with herbs which were useful in curing minor illnesses.

Look on the bright side

A strong faith in God allowed the settlers to face both illness and death with courage. In times of illness, a good sense of humor and a positive attitude to life helped. The settlers believed that "an ounce of prevention is worth a pound of cure." They lived simple lives.

Mother Nature was on the settlers' side. She gave them plenty of sunshine, fresh air, and a chance to grow nutritious food, such as wheat.

Kill or cure?

Treating symptoms *Doctors did not know the causes of disease. They treated the* **symptoms,** *not the causes of disease. If this girl's pulse is high, the doctor will not cure the cause. He will give her medicine to bring her heartbeat back to normal.*

Dirty rats! *The settlers never thought that animals as small as rats could carry disease. They suspected pigs, cows, horses, and dogs of spreading disease. Rats came to the New World aboard ships. They brought disease ashore.*

Heat a fever *People who suffered from high fevers were kept hot under many layers of blankets. Today we know that the easiest way to bring a fever down is to take a cool bath.*

Staying dirty *People in the early days believed that bathing too often removed protective oils from a person's skin. It was thought that without these oils, a person was open to disease.*

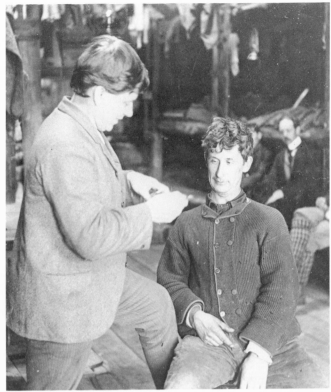

Bitter and better? The settlers thought that the more bitter a medicine, the better it would cure an illness. Settlers also wrongly believed that the more medicine they took, the faster they would get well.

Sick smells People thought diseases traveled through the air, the water, and under the ground. They associated diseases with a bad vapor called **miasma**. Doctors carried scented sticks which were supposed to stop the miasma from reaching the nose and entering the body.

The dark musties The settlers did not allow fresh air or sunlight into a sick person's room. They felt that the cold, fresh air made people sicker.

Lying around Those who were ill were told to stay in bed. The settlers did not realize how important a little exercise was to recovery.

Why would anyone stick a hand into a leech jar? Perhaps this apothecary's apprentice is petting her favorite leech!

Anthony has stepped on a thorn. It has gone into his foot. A poultice will help to draw out the thorn and prevent an infection.

The most common treatments

Early doctors did not have many ways of treating a patient. They were not able to operate. Early medicines were little help. Bleeding, blistering, plastering, and amputation were the methods most commonly used by doctors. Whether the disease was minor or serious, the settlers often relied on **phlebotomy** as a remedy. Phlebotomy was better known as "bleeding" or "bloodletting." The settlers thought that it was "bad blood" which contained the illness. Bloodletting made "bad blood" leave the body.

Hungry for blood

There were several ways to bleed a patient. One way was to apply **leeches** or bloodsuckers to a vein. First, a leech was placed in a thin tube. The patient's skin was washed and shaved. Then, the tube was turned over the vein. A drop of milk or blood was placed on the spot to encourage the leech to bite. The leech sucked blood from the vein. Once enough blood had been taken, the leech was sprinkled with salt. The salt forced the leech to stop sucking the blood and let go of the skin.

The same leeches were used many times. They were kept in a jar by the doctor, blacksmith, barber, or apothecary. In many communities any of these people would bleed patients. Barber advertised bloodletting as part of their business. Have you seen the red and white striped pole outside the barber shop? The colors on the pole originally stood for red blood and white bandages, the symbols of bloodletting.

Bleeding could be done with a **lancet.** When patients were cut with this small knife, they would bleed. In later years, a small box called a **scarificator** was invented. It contained small, sharp blades and was used to scratch a section of the patient's skin. A cup was heated and inverted over the scratches. A **vacuum** was created which caused the blood to flow freely from the vein. This procedure was called **cupping.**

Taking too much

Bleeding was a popular remedy. The settlers used it as a solution to many of their health problems. Unfortunately, what it really did was weaken the patient. The weaker the patient, the less chance for recovery. Today many people give blood so it can be used to make others well. Giving blood is not dangerous when only a certain amount is taken from the donor. However, the amount of blood that was taken from a patient in early days was much greater. Doctors bled patients until they fainted!

Another serious problem in bloodletting was the use of unclean instruments. Doctors did not know about germs, so they did not **sterilize** their medical instruments. Unclean medical tools were homes to germs. When these instruments were used, the germs spread to the patients and caused infections. The infections were treated by more bleeding, which meant that dirty instruments were used again! Doctors sometimes used the same tools on humans and animals. The tools were wiped clean of visible dirt, but the invisible germs remained.

Plasters and poultices

Plasters and poultices were used as remedies for many ailments. **Plasters** were mixtures that felt like paste. They were applied to the chest or back of a patient who had a chest cold or an internal pain. **Poultices** were made from bread and milk. Other ingredients, such as onions, potatoes, linseed oil, and herbs, were added. Poultices were placed on cuts, bites, wounds, and boils. One settler claimed that plasters made with cow manure cured everything from pneumonia to broken bones.

Early surgery

In the early days there were no anesthetics. **Surgery** was impossible to perform when the patient was awake. The only operation that early doctors dared to perform was **amputation.** When a doctor amputated, he cut off a patient's arm or leg. The patient was usually given wine to drink before the operation. The wine only helped to block out part of the pain. The limb was cut off with a saw. The saw was not sterilized, so the patient often got an infection. When the amputation was finished, the doctor **cauterized** the veins and arteries. He used hot tar to seal the limb so that it would not bleed.

This boy cracked his head. Will he be bled, plastered, or punished for getting into a fight?

Blistering

Another popular early medical practice was **blistering.** An acid was applied to the skin. The acid burned the skin, forming a blister. Sometimes hot pokers were used to cause the blister.

In the early days it was believed that the body could contain only one illness at a time. When a second illness entered the body, the first illness had to leave. If the skin was made to blister while someone was ill, the settlers hoped that the burn would force the first illness from the body.

Blistering was used as a remedy for fever, arthritis, and serious diseases such as cholera. Many people believed that blistering was effective. Blistering did not cure diseases. It did, however, force the patient to concentrate on a new pain. Even today, some people pinch themselves when they are in pain. The pain of the pinch can take the mind away from the more serious pain which is present in the body.

This old herb doctor walked from town to town selling his herbs to people who did not grow their own supply. He not only sold the herbs. He also told his customers how to prepare remedies for ailments.

Nature's medicines

In the early days, there were few doctors on the frontier or in the backwoods. When settlers arrived at their land in the wilderness, they had to make sure they had medicine in case they came down with an illness. The settlers brought some herbs with them from Europe. They planted herbs and made their own medicines from them. **Herbs** were plants, roots, and bark that were beneficial because they were used for flavoring food and dyeing cloth, as well as for healing the sick.

There were two types of drugs made from herbs. One type was called **benefits.** Benefits were used to prevent illness. They were similar to the vitamins we buy today. **Simples** were used to cure a specific pain or illness. For example, if you have a headache, you take aspirin. Aspirin would be considered a "simple."

Potions and lotions

Many new herbs were found in the forest where the settlers lived. It was usually the job of the mother or grandmother of the household to learn about the local herbs. In the fall, groups of women went deep into the woods by moonlight to gather herbs for the medicine chest. If you were to walk into the home of a settler in October or November, you would see bundles of herbs hanging from the ceiling in front of the fireplace. The herbs were hung up to dry. From these herbs came powders for pills, tonics for strength, plasters and poultices for pains and infections, teas for bad nerves, and lotions for the complexion. Many of the herbs used by the settlers can be found in our vitamins and drugs today.

Benefits and simples

The herbs in the following chart were used as both benefits and simples. A benefit prevents an illness. A simple relieves an illness. Families had their own recipes for making herbal remedies. Many people today still rely on herbs to make them feel better. Many of these herbs are sold in health-food stores.

Herb	Benefit	Cure or Relief of
alfalfa	▶ *good for pituitary gland*	▶ *arthritic pain*
bayberry bark	▶ *prevents hemorrhages*	▶ *congestion*
bee pollen	▶ *energy food*	▶ *allergies*
beet root	▶ *cleans liver and spleen*	▶ *sluggish liver*
black walnut hulls	▶ *good for nerves*	▶ *tapeworms*
burdock root	▶ *soothes kidneys*	▶ *impurities from blood*
catnip herb	▶ *soothes nerves*	▶ *colic in babies*
celery seeds		▶ *rheumatism*
comfrey leaves		▶ *diarrhea*
dandelion root (raw)	▶ *prevents anemia (high iron content)*	▶ *bladder and kidney problems*
fennel seed	▶ *takes away appetite*	▶ *gas, gout, colic*
garlic	▶ *stimulates digestive system*	▶ *asthma, whooping cough, heart problems*
ginseng	▶ *energy*	▶ *low blood pressure*
hawthorn berries	▶ *heart disease*	▶ *(restores) heart muscle wall*
horehound		▶ *sore throat*
horsetail	▶ *youthful skin*	▶ *kidney stones*
parsley	▶ *prevents growth of cancer cells*	▶ *(expels) gallstones*
red clover	▶ *blood purifier, prevents cancer*	
rosehips	▶ *prevents scurvy (high Vitamin C content)*	▶ *infection*
sage	▶ *cleans ulcers*	▶ *hemorrhaging*
wild lettuce		▶ *headaches, nervous tension*
willow bark		▶ *general pain*

Jessica is ill. She has had severe stomach cramps for days. Her parents have brought her to the nearby Indian village. The Indian doctor knows how to treat her dysentery. Jessica clings to her friend, the Chief, for comfort. She hopes the medicine will make her feel better.

Indian remedies

How did the settlers learn about the local herbs? They could not risk gathering and testing plants that might have been poisonous. The settlers learned about the local herbs from the Indians who lived in the area.

Aspirin from willow bark

The Indians taught the settlers how to treat fevers, intestinal worms, dysentery, and other disorders of the stomach and intestines. They discovered that chewing the inside bark of the willow tree made their pains less severe. Today, our aspirin is made from this substance. The bark of the slippery elm tree, an Indian discovery, is still used in medicines made for relief of stomach upset.

First aid

Indians were particularly successful treating snakebites, poisoning, fractures, dislocations, and wounds. They used a poultice of boiled spruce for removing embedded arrowheads. The Indians cleaned the wound and then sewed it up with a fiber taken from the inner bark of basswood or from the long tendon of a deer's leg.

Sweating out sickness

Many maladies were treated by making a patient perspire in a sweat-house. A tent or teepee was closed tightly. Hot stones were placed in the center and drenched with water. A thick steam formed inside the tent. The patient sat in the tent near the rocks. When covered with sweat, the patient was plunged into cold water and given a vigorous rubdown. A long nap followed.

The terrible toxins

Many people today take sauna baths regularly. Saunas are healthful because sweating gets rid of some of the **toxins** in our bodies. Toxins are dangerous poisons produced by bacteria. These toxins can store up in our bodies and can make us ill. The Indian remedy of sweating regularly was a good way of ridding the body of toxins, and thereby preventing some diseases.

The berries of the sumac tree were loaded with vitamin C. The Indians chewed these or made a nutritious tea from them.

This patient has spent time in a sweat-house. He has been plunged into cold water and rubbed down. Now he sleeps peacefully as the doctor prays for his recovery.

Grandma Martin tells the villagers about Gregory's injury. A bee has stung his arm and caused a huge red bump. Grandma has mixed a plaster of cow manure, dirt, and saliva to bring down the swelling. Gregory is not so sure that it will work. The Robinson sisters think that Grandma's remedy is horrible! Do you think it will help Gregory?

Ague Kill a chicken and hold its body against the bare feet of the patient. Have the patient swallow a cobweb rolled into a ball.

Common sense or nonsense?

Many of the herbs the settlers used are still valuable to medicine today. Herbs, however, were not the only remedies used. Other medical treatments had nothing to do with common sense. They were based on superstition. **Folk medicine** formulas were passed down through families. Sometimes the patients got better simply because they thought they would be cured. The following are samples of remedies, treatments, and cures that were believed to work. You be the judge!

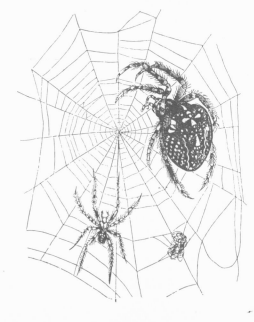

Scarlet Fever Put a piece of saffron in an onion and bake the onion until it is juicy. Feed the onion to the child.

Whooping Cough The father of the family should place the head of the sick child into a hole in a meadow for a few minutes at dusk. No other family member should be present.

Croup Make a mixture of garlic and oil from pigs' feet. Rub it into the patient's feet. Add skunk oil, if available. Apply leeches to the top of the body.

Cold Mix together goose grease and turpentine. Rub a large amount of it onto the patient's chest.

Tuberculosis Smoke dried cow dung. Inhale the fumes through a pipe.

Teething Hang the foot of a mole around the neck of the teething infant. Apply leeches behind the baby's ears. Cut the gums of the infant with a lancet to allow the teeth to come through easily.

Would you trust this doctor's advice on teething?

Cough and Sore Throat Simmer a piece of salt pork in hot vinegar and let the meat cool. Fasten the pork around the patient's neck with a piece of red flannel. If you have no pork, tie a dirty sock around the patient's neck.

15

People did not brush their teeth every day. They couldn't! There were no toothbrushes in the early day
People used small pieces of flannel and salt to clean their teeth once a week. Some people "brushed"
with a piece of wood splintered at the end. For extra cleaning, they dipped the splinters into gunpowde
Few people still had their teeth after the age of thirty. No wonder many people are interested in this
traveling toothbrush salesman. He promises the crowd that this new-fangled device will keep them fro
losing their teeth. It looks as if he is too late to help the old woman on the left.

Those dirty settlers!

The settlers did not have the same standards of cleanliness that we have today. There were three reasons for this. The settlers did not have running water in their homes. Water had to be brought in from a stream, well, or pump and heated for bathing and for washing clothes. Keeping clean was hard work! The second reason was that people in those days believed that bathing too often was unhealthy. One settler explained that it was just as unnatural for a person to bathe as it was to rub a fish in dirt. Thirdly, soap, toothpaste, and creams had to be made by the settlers themselves. People were careful not to use too much of these materials so that they would last as long as possible.

The pioneers made soap from animal fat and lye. They made toothpaste from a mixture of bark, myrrh, chalk, orris root, and sugar. Some people polished their teeth once a week by brushing them with gunpowder. Mouthwashes were made of lemon juice, wine, quinine, and cologne water.

Hair was washed with soap instead of shampoo. It was washed as seldom as possible, about once or twice a month. If a person had dandruff, bran was rubbed into the scalp. Settlers treated baldness by rubbing their heads with onions.

After water was used to wash the floor or to do laundry, it was thrown outside the door of the house or shanty. The dirty water seeped into the ground and contaminated the water in the well. Sometimes rats and other small animals fell into open wells, such as the one in this picture. This also spread disease.

These children have not had a bath in weeks. Their clothes are dirty and tattered. Their hair is uncombed. Not all children were this dirty. However, the picture shows that the settlers were certainly not a spotless bunch!

The settlers did keep their feet cleaner than the rest of their bodies. They usually washed their feet before going to bed. This boy found a way to keep his toes cool: air-conditioned socks!

Girls wanted to have long hair. They called it their "crowning glory." They brushed their hair each day. However, they felt washing the hair damaged it. They washed their hair about once a month.

Paul has never heard of nutrition. He eats a dinner of cake and pickles. He feels that as long as he is full, it does not matter what he eats. The combination of the food and the mystery he is reading is sure to give him some great nightmares!

The ABCs of nutrition

Many settlers did not have nutritious diets. They did not know that different foods affected the body in different ways. They were not able to get a variety of fruit, vegetables, meat, dairy products, and grains at all times of the year. During the winter months there were few fresh vegetables or fruit available. The settlers lived on a diet of meat, potatoes, and bread. They lacked important vitamins, such as vitamin C.

C-ing the scurvy cure

Many settlers became ill in the winter. They came down with a disease called **scurvy.** People thought that scurvy was due to a diet of too much salted meat. The truth was that scurvy was due to a lack of vitamin C. Scurvy caused the gums to swell and become bloody. The teeth fell out. Other symptoms of scurvy were exhaustion, sores on the arms and legs, and swelling of the muscles.

Sailors often suffered from scurvy. James Lind was a doctor in the Royal Navy. In 1753, he discovered that sailors who ate some fresh fruit or drank lemon juice every day did not develop scurvy. However, no one paid attention to Dr. Lind's discovery until about twenty years later. Captain Cook started a three-year voyage around the world in 1772. He kept his men healthy by stocking his ship with fresh fruit at every stop that he made. Not a single one of his sailors got scurvy. After Cook's success, many ships carried a cargo of lemons and oranges.

Early settlers in this country could not always get fresh fruit. How did they prevent scurvy? The Indians taught the settlers how to solve this problem. Indians rarely got scurvy because they chewed on the inner bark of the juniper tree. The bark contained vitamin C. The red berries of the sumac tree also contained **ascorbic acid** or vitamin C. The berries could be chewed raw or made into a tea.

Vitamin D-ficiencies

Vitamins are necessary for the body to grow properly. Lack of a vitamin is called a vitamin **deficiency.** Vitamin deficiencies were harmful to children. Young children who did not get enough vitamin D or **calcium** in their diets suffered from **rickets.** Healthy bones could not form and grow without these nutrients. The bones became soft and deformed. Children with rickets became bowlegged or knock-kneed. After the bones were deformed, they could not be fixed, even though the disease went away.

The settlers thought that the more they ate, the healthier they would become. From the time they were born, children were fed an unbalanced diet. People thought that a gruel made of bread and water was more healthful than milk. They fed this gruel or **pap** to children whenever they cried. It was not nutritious.

The importance of vitamins

The early scientists did not understand that it is important to eat a well-balanced diet. They did not realize that people must eat a variety of foods. Later, scientists understood that there were special ingredients in foods that were necessary for health. They called these ingredients "accessory food factors." We call them vitamins! Today we know the importance of vitamins and a well-balanced diet.

A pot full of health

Some of the early settlers were lucky. They discovered that eating certain foods made them look and feel better. In the following story, a woman tells her neighbors about the drink that makes her children so healthy.

Mrs. Samuels lived in a small farm community. She had a strong husband and three healthy young children. Joan, Peter, and Elaine spent the morning at school, did chores in the afternoon, and still had energy to play games and have fun in the evening. The children were hardly ever tired. The other parents in the community were amazed by the Samuels children.

One fine summer evening the settler women gathered for an apple bee. This was the time to gossip and exchange useful information. Just as the bee was ending, Mrs. Schmidt spoke up. "Mrs. Samuels, this has been puzzling us for a long time. Your children have such shiny hair and rosy cheeks. They are always laughing. How do you manage to keep them so healthy?"

Mrs. Samuels smiled. She was very fond of her neighbors. She was amused that it had taken them so long to ask for her secret. "I make sure that my children drink a tall glass of pot liquor each day," she said to the women. Mrs. Samuels did not have to wait long to see the effect of her remark. The women were horrified that Mrs. Samuels would give her young children liquor to drink. How could liquor make anyone healthy?

Mrs. Samuels listened to the shocked whispers. Then she could no longer keep from laughing. "My friends," she giggled, "let me explain my secret a little better. When I boil turnips in our big tin pot, the water that remains in the pot is very tasty. This water is the pot liquor that my children drink! It seems to keep them in high spirits!" The women blushed at their foolishness. They should have known better. "Thank you for the tip," they grinned. "We will never throw our pot 'liquor' away again!"

Mrs. Samuels did not know it, but she had introduced her friends to a good source of vitamin A. Today we know that vitamin A helps us to have shiny hair and clear skin.

Babies were not given a good nutritious start in life. They were fed a mixture of bread and water. During teething they were given bread crusts to chew.

These children are enjoying the warm milk that came straight from the cow. This milk might contain bacteria which could make them ill. Pasteurization has not yet been invented.

Grain, which provided bread for the settlers, also gave them alcohol. Alcohol hurt those who drank. It destroyed their family life. This drinker is no longer able to feed or care for his family.

Food or poison?

Milk is an important part of a good diet. It is especially good for children. It contains many of the vitamins and minerals that children need in order to grow. In the early days, there were problems with milk. Milk was sometimes dangerous to drink. It contained bacteria that could cause diseases, such as scarlet fever, typhoid fever, diphtheria, and bovine tuberculosis. Bovine tuberculosis damaged children's bones and joints. Milk was not **pasteurized** in the early days. Pasteurization was invented by Louis Pasteur in the later part of the nineteenth century. You can see how pasteurization got its name. Pasteurizing milk means heating milk to just below its boiling point. This process kills the bacteria but saves most of the nutrients.

The people who lived in the bigger towns and cities had other problems with their milk. Dishonest shopkeepers put chalk and plaster mixed with water into milk, to make it seem as if they had more to sell. There were no government regulations to stop merchants from adding dangerous products to milk and other foods.

Settlers could not depend on the safety of their food, either. Merchants also added extra ingredients, such as sawdust, to the foods they sold. People often bought sour butter and diseased meat and fish.

Too much food and drink

Those people who had good food often ate too much of it. **Gout** was a disease that was most common among rich people who ate many rich foods. People with gout had too much **uric acid** in their blood. Gout was similar to arthritis. It made the joints of the bones swell. It deformed the hands and feet. People with gout had trouble walking.

Many people had terrible table manners. They gulped their food down too quickly. Indigestion was their constant companion. Many people suffered from this condition.

Some of the settlers also drank too much alcohol. This caused heart trouble, liver ailments, and worst of all, family problems. Alcoholism was dangerous, not only to the drinker, but also to his or her family. Alcoholics ruined their health and their family life.

These people are buying contaminated milk. Distilleries produced alcohol. Many distilleries also kept cows and sold their milk. The cows were fed a mash made from garbage and whiskey. The alcohol was in the cow's milk. When babies drank milk from these cows, they became tipsy.

Alcohol causes people to mistreat the ones they should love. This unfortunate baby is badly neglected. His life is miserable. He gets little nourishment or attention.

John's morning chore is to fetch water for his family. Pails filled with water are heavy and harmful to John's back and growing bones.

The dangers of settler life

Exercise is important for a healthy body and a sound mind. Exercise was certainly something most of the early settlers did not lack. Most of the settlers were farmers. Farm work involved physical labor, such as carrying water, chopping wood, plowing fields, and stooking hay.

Farm life was hard on the delicate bones of children. Farm children had many chores. They had to carry water from the well. Water is heavy! Sometimes children carried water in buckets attached to yokes which hung from their shoulders. Children had to chop firewood. Sometimes they lost fingers when they used the sharp axes.

Working in a farmhouse was backbreaking. Farm women had to lift heavy iron pots in and out of the fireplace. When stoves were invented, the settlers faced another health problem. The stoves smoked so much that people coughed and choked. They breathed polluted air. Women who spent most of their days indoors cooking, cleaning, and washing, suffered the most.

Smoke and fire

Fire was a big problem in farm and city homes. If the stovepipes were not properly cleaned, a fire could start without a moment's notice. People had to be careful to keep clothing, curtains, and tablecloths away from the candle flames. Outside the home, fires were caused when the settlers tried to burn trees to make room for fields. Sometimes the wind shifted, blowing the flames in the direction of the house or forest. Long periods of hot, dry weather also caused bush and prairie fires.

Snakes were a menace in the fields. One day two small boys were sent out to cut underbrush. A snake bit one of the boys on the hand. The boy did not panic. He knew that the only way he could stay alive was to act quickly. He ordered his younger brother to chop his hand off immediately. The little boy started to cry. He could not bring himself to hurt his brother! The older boy repeated the order. "Chop my hand off this very minute, for if you wait, I shall surely die!" This time the little boy acted without hesitation. He did not want his brother to die. The boy without the hand lived to a ripe old age.

Outside farm work was tiring. Father wipes his brow. The children have helped him all day. What's that in the distance? It looks like fire. Father and the children are worried that if the wind changes, the fire may reach their farm.

Fire was a danger both outside and inside the house. James accidentally knocked a candle over and his sleeve caught fire. Stop, drop, and roll, James!

Howls in the dark

Animals were a constant threat to the settlers. Bears and wolves killed and ate the settlers' chickens, sheep, and pigs. Settlers who traveled were especially afraid of wolves. There are no records of wolves killing any settlers, but there are many stories about wolves scaring people half to death!

A girl of sixteen was sent on horseback with a bag of corn, to have it ground at the mill. It was midnight before the corn was ground and the girl could begin her journey home. As her horse trotted along the path under the spreading trees, the girl was startled by the distant sound of yelps and barks. The howls grew nearer and nearer. She urged her horse to its fastest speed. At times, the wolves were so close that when she looked back, the girl could see their evil eyes gleaming through the darkness. She went on as fast as her horse could carry her, running from death. At last, exhausted, she reached the door of her home. The bag of precious food was still full.

Little wonder that the settlers were so afraid of wolves. How would you like to be followed home by this vicious-looking creature?

The whole Fredrick family has come down with influenza. They are too ill even to feed themselves. Fortunately, one of Mary's school friends and her mother have decided to visit. They are shocked to see everyone so ill. They will bring food so the Fredricks will not starve.

The familiar diseases

Many diseases produced the same symptoms of fever, vomiting, headaches, and coughing. Often doctors had problems **diagnosing** diseases for this reason. To give a diagnosis, a doctor had to look at all the symptoms and then decide which disease caused them.

Ague or influenza?

Books and diaries written by settlers are filled with stories of people who suffered from a disease that they called **ague.** When we have a fever or a cold, we often say that we have the "flu." We are not really sure of the exact name of our illness, but flu is a useful name for our symptoms. In the days of the settlers, ague was used in the same way as the word flu is used today. Many of the settlers who thought they had ague really had **influenza.** The patient suffered from fever, chills, aches and pains, nosebleeds, and a cough.

Chills, fever and sweat

Settlers described what they called an attack of ague in the following way. It began with several hours of fever, followed by severe chills and sweating. These stages alternated for hours days, or weeks. Sometimes a whole family came down with it at once. The following is the story of how one family survived.

"Joseph and his wife were attacked with ague. Having no neighbors, they were forced to rely on themselves. Their illness was so severe that they had to remain helpless in bed. For three days and three nights, they had no food or fire, and they realized that they would die. Suddenly, a band of Indians arrived. The Indian women tenderly nursed their white brother and sister. They gave them food, and applied simple but effective remedies. Meanwhile, the men cut the corn in the settlers' small field and stored it in a log shack. Joseph and his wife would have food this winter and would be alive to eat it, thanks to the Indians!"

Catarrh was a common settler complaint. It was like a bad cold. The settlers must have had a heavy feeling in their noses. The tonic that was advertised promised to lighten the pressure.

What this settler couple called ague was probably **malaria**. Mosquitoes carried the parasites that caused malaria. This disease was common near swamps and rotting vegetation. Sometimes malaria patients seemed to recover from the disease, but the parasites stayed in their blood. The symptoms returned again and again. Today we only hear of malaria in tropical countries. It is no longer common in North America.

Pneumonia, catarrh, and bilious upsets

Other common ailments were pneumonia, spotted fever, bilious headaches, dysentery, and catarrh. **Pneumonia** is an inflammation of the lungs. It has many different symptoms and was easily confused with other diseases. Pneumonia was often the result of another disease. When a settler came down with a bad cold, the cold sometimes developed into pneumonia.

Catarrh was a common word used by the settlers to describe an illness. A person with catarrh usually had a sore throat, a cough, difficulty in breathing, and **laryngitis**. Catarrh was also used to describe stomach trouble. One could have catarrh of the stomach due to a bad diet. It was associated with mucus in the body. Catarrh meant everything from a cold to an upset stomach.

The term **bilious** was often used by the settlers. People believed that illnesses were a result of body fluids being out of balance. Bilious means having too much **bile**. Settlers believed that too much of this fluid, which is produced in the liver, caused headache, upset stomach, vomiting, and diarrhea.

25

Visiting time at the hospital! Children a hundred years ago were not as healthy as children today. They came down with many childhood diseases, such as the mumps, measles, scarlet fever, and diphtheria.

Childhood illnesses

Most diseases affected people of all ages, but there were several that affected young children in particular. Most children were attacked by the **mumps** virus. They developed fevers and swollen glands below the ears. Mumps was an infectious disease, which meant children could easily catch it from each other.

Measles was also extremely infectious. The child was covered with red spots. Measles was dangerous because it weakened the body. Children could develop infections in their lungs.

Chicken pox was similar to measles. It was contagious. Children caught chicken pox from other children. Itchy red sores appeared on the skin.

Scarlet fever was often confused with measles. It resulted in a high fever, a sore throat, and a red rash on the skin. It sometimes left children with weakened hearts.

Whooping cough was a disease especially dangerous to infants. A membrane grew along the air passages which made it hard for the child to breathe. The victim would cough and then draw in air with a peculiar, loud "whoop." Fortunately, whooping cough, like measles, seldom occurred more than once in a lifetime.

Poliomyelitis or polio was a terrible disease. It attacked the spinal cord and the brain. A child could wake up one morning and discover that she had polio. Any or all of the child's limbs could be paralyzed. Only rest in bed could help lessen the effects of the disease.

Finding a cure for diphtheria

Diphtheria was a common childhood disease. A thick, gray **membrane** formed inside the throat. This made it difficult for the child to breathe. Often the child died of a weakened heart caused by the diphtheria.

A German scientist named Robert Koch studied this disease. He learned that diphtheria bacteria or **bacilli** could be found only in samples from a patient's throat. The diphtheria, however, was somehow affecting the heart of the diseased victim. Koch concluded correctly that the bacilli must produce a poisonous substance, a **toxin.** This toxin circulated through the body and damaged the cells of the heart.

Having the mumps must have felt as if your mouth was filled with marbles. Gary feels a lot of pain. His medicine has not helped much.

Two medical students grew diphtheria bacteria. They strained out the bacilli. The toxin was left. They injected guinea pigs with the toxin, and the animals died. When they injected the guinea pigs with a small amount of toxin, the animals had a mild attack of diphtheria. They lived, and were again injected. The second time, they did not become infected with diphtheria.

The experiments continued. Blood from a guinea pig that had diphtheria was mixed with toxin. The mixture was injected into a healthy guinea pig. The healthy animal did not become sick. The infected blood acted as an **antitoxin.** The antitoxin prevented diphtheria. When this antitoxin was injected into a guinea pig that already had the disease, the guinea pig was cured. The antitoxin both prevented and cured the disease.

Disabling diseases

Many children lost the use of their legs through diseases, such as polio and tuberculosis. Some, such as the boy in the wheelchair, had their legs amputated. These children are learning to deal with their disabilities at this hospital school.

These twins enjoy each other's company. They were born with bowed legs. Casts have been put on their legs so that the legs will grow straight.

This orphaned boy must walk with crutches. He must search for food and a place to sleep. There were no services to help such children.

This craftsman specializes in making shoes with braces for victims of spinal tuberculosis. These shoes will help to support the children's legs.

These boys have tuberculosis. The disease has changed the shapes of their bodies. They wear special shoes, which help them to walk.

Grandma Jones has spent most of her life in a wheelchair. She had polio as a child. She does not just sit around, however. She is well known for the beautiful pottery she makes.

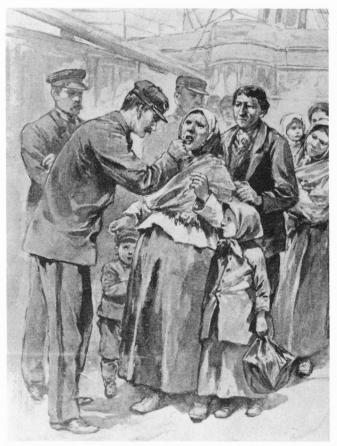

The immigration officer checks this woman's mouth to see if she has a "furry" tongue. Immigrants who looked ill were quarantined until they were well again.

Dirty, crowded ships often caused passengers to catch typhus and cholera. These citizens are afraid the passengers will cause an epidemic.

This poor immigrant woman may have cholera. She is being taken from her apartment. The ambulance will take her to a quarantine hospital.

Epidemics

Epidemic diseases threatened the lives of early settlers. Epidemic diseases were contagious. They spread from person to person. Some epidemics were caused by infected food. Others were caused by rats. An epidemic disease could infect many people at once.

Influenza, typhus, typhoid fever, and smallpox were contagious diseases. One of the most dreaded diseases was **cholera.** There were different types of cholera, but all had severe symptoms. The victims suffered from nausea, vomiting, chills, thirst, and spasms. The blood circulated slowly. When the skin began to appear bluish and shrunken, death was near.

Contagious cholera

Cholera was caused by a **bacillus.** Bacilli could contaminate water supplies. Bacilli were also carried by flies. The early doctors did not know this. They tried to treat cholera by bleeding, blistering, or cupping. They thought that feeding milk to patients could cure

The early city streets were often dirty, carrying deadly germs. People started to suspect that one way of getting rid of disease was to clean cities and find better ways of getting rid of garbage and human waste. They soon found out they were right. There were fewer outbreaks of cholera in clean cities.

the illness. Some people believed that you would catch cholera if you were afraid of it. Others believed that comets, the sun, the moon, or too much oxygen in the atmosphere caused a cholera epidemic. Some settlers pointed at fruit and vegetables as the causes of cholera. They stopped eating these foods.

Quarantined!

The people who believed that cholera epidemics were related to the arrival of immigrants were correct. The ships that brought settlers to this country were so unclean and crowded that many immigrants suffered from cholera. In some places immigrants had to pay a medical tax before they were allowed to land. This tax was used to pay for medical services and cholera treatment. Often local residents held public demonstrations. They refused to let ships land if they suspected that the immigrants on board carried cholera. These immigrants were confined to a hospital. This isolation was called a **quarantine.** Quarantines often did not prevent the spread of the disease.

People prayed that they would not get diseases. They were terrified of smallpox, cholera, and typhus. Sometimes prayer was the only hope.

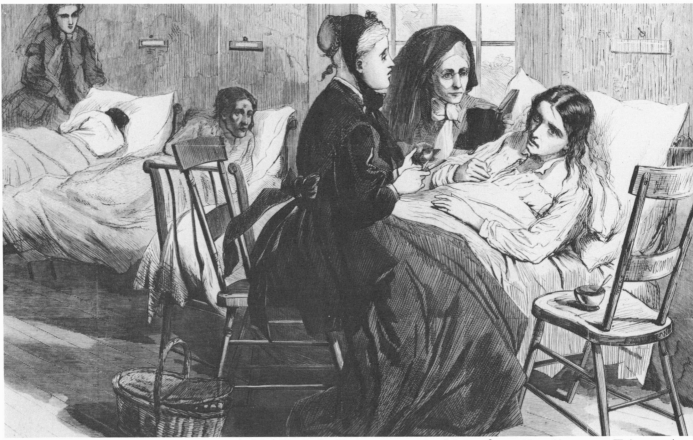

These tuberculosis patients are very ill. Their bodies are wasting away from the disease. This man's wife tries to cheer him up with an apple and a cup of soup. The nurse reads to him from the Bible.

Patients who had tuberculosis were isolated in shacks, such as the one above. Visitors came to see them. During the day the patients are taken out into the sunshine and fresh air.

Tuberculosis

Tuberculosis was also called "consumption."
Consumption meant that the body tissue
was wasting away. This is what happened
to the tuberculosis victim. The patient's
body tissue was destroyed by the tuberculosis
bacteria. **Tubercles** were fine granules barely
visible to the human eye. They grew in any
organ of the body, even in the lungs and the
brain. The tubercles multiplied and changed
in such a way that they damaged or destroyed
the organ. Often the result was death.

Bacteria everywhere

Tuberculosis was a contagious disease. People
did not realize this until late in the nineteenth
century. How did the bacteria enter the body?
There were three possible ways. Bacteria
could be carried in milk and other foods. It
could be carried in the saliva of a tuberculosis
victim. Bacteria also lived in the air. When
people with tuberculosis coughed or spat,
the air or ground carried the bacteria. If
other people inhaled the air or the dust, they
could be infected. Spitting became a crime
punished by a stiff penalty because tuberculosis
bacteria lived for a long time in the dirt.
The bacteria was killed only by direct sunlight.

Desperate measures

Some people believed that tuberculosis was
a punishment from God. Most doctors believed
that tuberculosis could not be cured. Some
quacks prescribed strange "remedies." These
are some examples. Smoke cow dung. Eat
butter made from the cream of cows that
graze in churchyards. Drink elephant's blood
and milk. Eat mice boiled in salt and oil.
Of course these were ridiculous suggestions,
but tuberculosis victims were desperate enough
to try anything.

Fresh air and plenty of rest

The early healing center, or **sanitarium,** was
probably useful in helping the tuberculosis
victims. The sanitorium provided patients
with fresh air and rest. Now we know that
tuberculosis is common among people who
are badly housed and poorly fed. We know
that people with tuberculosis should be
isolated so that other people do not catch
the disease.

*These young victims of spinal tuberculosis met
each other at the hospital. They have become
good friends. Their lungs, spine, and bones
have been affected by their disease.*

Many children once caught tuberculosis from
contaminated milk. Today, **pasteurization**
kills the bacteria in milk. **Chemotherapy**
is now a successful treatment for tuberculosis,
but it only works if it is combined with rest,
good food, and fresh air. Vaccinations have
been invented to help protect people from
this disease.

Pasteurized milk.

Death was a sad part of settler life. These women grieve over the loss of their niece. They have come to comfort their brother. In the early days, people paid their respects at home, not at a funeral parlor.

Death

Today we can be thankful to many scientists and doctors who have discovered cures for the illnesses that killed many settlers. We can be thankful for good health care for adults and children. In the days of the settlers, sickness caused many deaths. The average settler was expected to live 30 years. Today, people are expected to live to be more than twice that age. Because there was little knowledge of the causes of diseases, there was little that people could do to fight serious illness.

Diseases and accidents were especially dangerous to children. The settlers were forced to accept that some of their children would not live long. Today it is hard for us to imagine that children might have to die at a young age. Many settler children died before they were five years old. The settlers grieved over their terrible losses. Most people were deeply religious. They believed that children were taken by God to a happier place. This belief made accepting death a little easier.

The danger of childbirth

Women also had a high death rate. Giving birth to a baby can be a natural, wonderful experience, but sometimes there are problems. Today, doctors can usually save the lives of the mother and child even when there are serious difficulties during birth. In earlier times, however, a mother and her baby often died when such difficulties occurred.

If you visit an old cemetery, you will find the gravestones of many children who died young. You will notice that one man often remarried several times. The harshness of life and the difficulties of giving birth without modern medical care caused the deaths of many women. Everyone suffered. The miracle of medicine is its power to prevent the sorrows that caused the settlers so much pain.

This mother has just given birth. She is very ill. The baby seems to be well. Grandmother is worried about both of them.

Most of the settlers were religious. This mother is heartbroken about her baby's death, but she believes her child has gone to Heaven.

Early doctors made house calls. This physician was on his way to visit a sick patient when he was stopped by a traveler. The traveler wants the doctor to give him a diagnosis.

The early doctors

Today it is hard work to become a doctor. Students must pass difficult exams to get into medical school. They must study for many years and work as interns in hospitals. In the days of the early settlers, the medical students often did not go to school to learn to become doctors. They learned about medicine by working for other doctors. This learning period was called an apprenticeship. Medical apprentices had many duties. They cared for the doctors' horses, swept the offices, ran errands, delivered messages, mixed plasters, and gathered herbs. After years of being doctors' servants, they eventually called themselves doctors. They were not required to pass difficult exams. They did not need diplomas. When a doctor felt his student was ready to work on his own, that student was then called a "doctor."

Patients beware!

Ministers were among the first doctors. Innkeepers, schoolteachers, and even butchers acted as doctors. These people were not trained doctors. Certainly, they had never read books about medicine! These "doctors" learned by doing. Doctors who were educated in the medical schools in Europe probably were not better doctors than those who learned medicine in the early settlements.

Doctors often could not make people well. Sometimes they made people sicker than they were before they were treated. The settlers did not always trust doctors. Often the settlers looked after their own illnesses. Doctors who settled in communities sometimes could not earn enough from "doctoring" alone. They had to be farmers or merchants too.

The village doctor was usually the apothecary as well. Doctors mixed and gave medicines to their patients. Some of these medicines were made of herbs. Some contained dangerous ingredients, such as mercury. Calomel, another name for mercury chloride, was prescribed as a remedy for many ailments. Large enough doses of mercury can cause death. No wonder so many patients felt worse instead of better. Doctors used gold, silver, and precious stones as remedies. Ground pearls were thought to be particularly useful in treating diseases of the eye.

Personal attention

There was a good side to being a country doctor. The doctor's patients were friends and neighbors. He delivered many of the babies in the community and watched them grow up. The country doctor really cared for the patients who needed his help. When they were ill, the doctor stayed with them for as long as he was needed. Sometimes he looked after the animals of his patients. Often he was also the village veterinarian.

A poultry wage

In the early days, few people went to the doctor's office. Doctors made house calls. Sometimes they charged the patient according to the distance they had to ride. Few settlers could afford to pay doctors in money. Doctors were often paid with chickens, eggs, meat, or vegetables. Today, few doctors make house calls. When we are ill, we go to the doctor's office or a clinic. We usually don't know our doctor very well. In the days of the settlers, the loving concern of the country doctor helped to make up for his lack of knowledge about medicine.

This country doctor was also the minister.

Inside the apothecary

Enter the mysterious world of the **apothecary** shop. Let your eyes drink in the colors of the many jars containing strange and powerful potions. Allow your nostrils to be thrilled by pounded aromatic roots and spices mingled with the smell of liniments and antiseptics. Discover powders scented with violets and roses. Brace your nostrils for the occasional whiffs of poison! Notice the gold labels bearing strange symbols, not just pasted on but burned into the glass. Peek into the wooden drawers and wonder at the curious contents. Examine the rows of ointment pots and glass medicine phials. Feel the cool smoothness of the marble mortar and pestle, the apothecary's most important instruments. Greet squirming leeches in a huge jar on the counter. Cross your fingers and hope that you never have to watch any of these creatures suck your blood!

The book of remedies

The drugs in the apothecary shop were made of roots, plants, berries, and bark. These medicinal plants were sometimes brought over from Europe. Often they were grown by the apothecary or collected from the countryside. Many of the apothecary's herbal remedies were written in a book called the **pharmacopoeia**. This book listed the names of the drugs and included instructions about their preparation and use. Some of these remedies were hundreds of years old. Many of these remedies were natural and useful. Often, however, they were based on false beliefs.

The sign of a cure

One popular theory was the **Doctrine of Signatures.** In this theory, the clues, or "signatures," to an illness were based on the shape or color of a plant. A plant was supposed to cure the part of the body that it looked like. Poppies, which are shaped like skulls, were thought to relieve diseases of the head. Walnuts were called "brain food" because they resembled the brain. The petals of the rose were supposed to be good for the blood because of their red color. People thought that almonds improved the eyesight. Can you guess why? The Signature theory is interesting, but has no value. What a plant looks like has nothing to do with its powers to cure.

Doubling as doctors

Whenever the early settlers felt ill and needed remedies, they headed for the apothecary shop. In the early days, apothecaries were also considered doctors. Their main job was to prepare remedies and treatments for patients. They also performed minor surgery, did amputations, and dressed wounds. Apothecaries were not as knowledgeable as doctors, but they charged less money for their services.

The apothecary's apprentice

There were no training schools for apothecaries. Someone who wished to learn the trade had to obtain a position as an apprentice. An apprentice received on-the-job training for a number of years. Beginners were given boring, simple jobs, such as sweeping. As time went on, they were given more responsibility.

Apprentices learned the formulas for all the remedies. Most of the necessary ingredients were plants that grew in local forests. Apprentices were trained to recognize these plants. It was their job to keep fresh supplies of these herbs. They learned to grind and mix ingredients for the remedies. Most apprentices also had accounting chores. They kept records of the patients who had not paid their bills. Apprentices were also taught to give treatments, such as bleeding and blistering. After their apprenticeships were over, the apprentices were able to open their own shops.

This apothecary is crushing berries in an early mortar and pestle made of wood. The mortar and pestles of the later apothecaries were made of marble or brass.

The apothecary looks at the contents of the jars. One of his clients has just asked him for a remedy for gout.

Hood's SARSA PA RILLA Cures

VOL. I, NO. 4   HOOD'S LABORATORY, LOWELL   U.S.A.   HOODS AND ONLY HOODS

A HERO OF BALAKLAVA.   BE SURE TO READ   O OBTAIN HOOD'S SARSAPARILLA.

One of the Last Three Survivors
of the Charge of the 600
Dies in New York.

A Medal Won in Fo___
Great Fi___

Dismounted ___
Riderless ___

A Policeman ___

Swelling in th___
Eight ___

All Other Prepar___
Hood's C___

When ___ Say

HOOD'S Sarsaparilla CURES

We make no idle or extravagant claim. The advertising of Hood's
Sarsaparilla is always within the bounds of reason, because it is

40

Patent medicines

Apothecaries made a good living in the early days of the nineteenth century. Many people went directly to the apothecary for treatment and medicine. Apothecaries charged less than doctors. However, patent medicines cost even less than the remedies made up by the apothecary.

Patent medicines appeared in the nineteenth century. Advances were being made in the printing process, and more newspapers were being published. To help pay the printing costs, publishers made room for advertisements on the newspaper pages. Many of the products advertised were patent medicines.

Secret ingredients

Most patent medicines were made from a "secret formula." To have the right or patent to make and sell such medicines, the owner had to give the formula to the government. Patent medicines were sometimes called tonics or nostrums. Each patent medicine was packaged in a special bottle or box. It was illegal for someone to duplicate a container that had been patented. Many patent medicines had fancy labels listing the benefits of the medicine.

In the advertisements, the promoters of patent medicines often criticized doctors. They tried to make doctors appear foolish. The best way to stay healthy, according to the patent advertisements, was not to visit the doctor. Instead, the advertisements said, the customers should buy the latest nostrum.

Nostrums claimed to cure consumption, headaches, backaches, and toothaches. Many nostrums were advertised as "cure-alls." They were supposed to be magic medicines that could cure every ailment.

Cure-alls cure nothing!

Many people believed that patent medicines worked. Unfortunately, most patented tonics were developed by **quacks,** who only wanted to fool the public and become rich. They claimed that their nostrums could even cure cholera and tuberculosis. Some patent medicines were quite harmful. Many contained dangerous drugs and large quantities of alcohol. Some nostrums contained as much as 35 per cent alcohol. That's a great deal of alcohol. Beer contains about 5 per cent alcohol.

THAT WISE OLD SAYING,

"An Ounce of Prevention is Worth a Pound of Cure," may well have been a prediction in reference to Scott's Emulsion, an ounce of which has frequently shown its worth in the production of a pound of healthy flesh.

A new saying, also applicable to Scott's Emulsion, might be that "A Pound of Cure is Worth a Ton of Relief," for sixteen ounces of this preparation has been known to create enough of healthy flesh to make all the difference between alarmingly low vitality and robust health. Relief is good—*Cure is better*.

SCOTT'S EMULSION

of Cod-Liver Oil with Hypophosphites of Lime and Soda is, above all things, *food*. In that word is included the best idea of *medicine*. And Scott's Emulsion is the best meaning of the word "food," in that it is the most nutritious of all fat-foods, and therefore the quickest builder of sound flesh.

Scott's Emulsion has done away with the objectionable features of cod-liver oil, bad taste and indigestibility—it can be taken and readily assimilated when even weak forms of fat-foods tax digestion; and this for the simple reason that Scott's Emulsion is fat *already partly digested*. It has been tested in all forms of wasting diseases, with results really magical. Nothing has done or can do so much for delicate children.

Prepared by SCOTT & BOWNE, Chemists, New York.

Sold by Druggists Everywhere. $1.00.

Scott's Emulsion can readily be distinguished from substituted and inferior preparations by means of its salmon-colored wrapper containing label of man with fish on back.

Read the words of this old advertisement. Do you believe that cod-liver oil is the "quickest builder of sound flesh"?

New regulations

Eventually, medical scientists began to examine the contents of various patent medicines. They discovered that a number of the tonics were not medicinal at all, but were cheap liquids which could cure nothing. Governments also began to investigate the formulas of patent medicines and to publish warnings about them. Early in the twentieth century, legal controls were introduced that regulated the quality of medicine. Soon, nostrums had to be medically proven before they could be patented. Today, the labels on all medicines must list the ingredients. Now, patent medicines are safe if used properly and under the direction of a doctor.

The phrenologist is checking the shape of this girl's skull. He "reads the bumps" on her head. He claim that he can tell her what her personality is like from the position and size of the bumps.

In the early days, some people blamed their illnesses on witches. These so-called "witches" were often women who were a little different from other people. Perhaps they showed more spirit than other women did. Many "witch hunts" were held. These women were put on trial, which sometimes involved the use of a "dunking stool." The woman was held under water. If she did not drown, she was found guilty, because only witches could breathe under water. The woman could not win. Guilty witches were burned at the stake. Many witch hunts took place in New England in the very early days. Laws were soon passed against them. However, many people continued to believe in witches.

Competing to cure

Country doctors and apothecaries had to compete for their share of patients. There were no government regulations about who was allowed to treat the sick. The community realized that doctors could not help patients recover from some ailments. When a serious epidemic broke out, such as cholera, people died by the thousands. People lost faith in doctors. They turned to other "healers" for hope.

Phrenologists

Phrenologists believed that the mind was made up of 40 different sections. Each of these sections controlled certain character-istics. The ability to imitate was located in one area of the brain. If that area of a person's head happened to be large, it meant that the individual was a good imitator. If the back of a person's head was large, that person was supposed to have very strong feelings. If the top of the head was well developed, the person was meant to become a minister, judge, or teacher.

Witchmasters

Some healers claimed that the devil caused illness through the work of witches. Some people believed that there were witches living among them. People thought these witches cast spells on people and made them sick. The only way to lift a spell was to hire a **witchmaster.** Witchmasters made a great deal of money because many of the settlers were superstitious. Witchmasters claimed that they could cast spells as well as remove them. If a witch cast a spell on a settler, a witchmaster offered to get rid of the spell, for a fee. Some medical doctors were also witchmasters. One country doctor was so superstitious that he hung horseshoes over his doors. He also set a trap by his bed, hoping to catch a witch.

43

The villagers flock into the local meeting hall. A faith healer is in town. They believe that if they pray with him, they will be cured.

This girl is trying to relieve her father's terrible toothache by putting oil of cloves on his tooth. He will probably have to visit the tooth-puller.

This man is being "mesmerized." Mesmerism was named after F. A. Mesmer. He claimed that his hypnotism could remove "bad spirits" from the body. People soon saw through him.

RESCUED FROM A BED OF SUFFERING
PARKERS TONIC brings the bloom of health to the cheek and delight to the heart.

Many quacks traveled the countryside selling quick cures. Some advertised their useless tonics in the newspapers.

Painful dentistry

The settlers did not take good care of their teeth. When they had toothaches, they lived with the pain until they could not bear it any longer. Then they had to find someone to fix or pull their teeth.

There were no laws about dentistry in the rural areas. Some communities had several "tooth-pullers." Almost anyone could advertise a tooth-pulling business. Some tooth-pullers even claimed that they could pull teeth without pain. Settlers had a large choice of tooth-pullers. The doctor, blacksmith, butcher, barber, and several farmers were all able to pull teeth.

Settlers usually had their bad teeth pulled out. First, the tooth-puller cut the gums around the teeth with a knife. Then he used an instrument called a turnkey to grab the bad teeth and yank them out. Many people who had their teeth pulled developed infections because the tools were not sterilized.

In many towns and cities, there were dentists who were able to fill teeth. The fillings were usually made of silver or gold. They were so expensive that not many people could afford them. The fact that there were no anesthetics also made settlers think twice about having a filling put in. Having a tooth drilled to make room for a filling took longer than having it pulled. It was less painful to get rid of the tooth than to save it with a filling. You can guess why settlers preferred to have their teeth yanked out!

Homeopaths

Homeopaths were popular healers in the nineteenth century. Some doctors killed their patients with medicines that they did not know were dangerous. People began to be more afraid of the cure than of the illness itself. They turned to homeopaths. Homeopaths believed that small doses of medicines were the best cures. They thought that watering down medicine and shaking it made the medicine more powerful because the "vital force" of that medicine was released. Some homeopaths diluted medicine with so much water that the "medicine" became little more than water. Many quacks, posing as homeopaths, traveled around the countryside selling tonics made of water and alcohol.

Homeopaths believed in the "hair of the dog" theory. If a dog bit a person, homeopaths thought that the best remedy was to apply a part of the dog to the wound. People pulled out the hairs of a mad dog, made a paste with them, and put the paste on the bite. If a person had a headache, the homeopath provided a medicine that actually caused headaches. This would be diluted with water. The treatment for the illness was based on its cause!

There was a good side to homeopathy. It showed people that drugs could be dangerous. Homeopaths did not harm as many people as doctors did with some of their poisonous cures. Homeopaths believed in a good diet and a clean body. These simple ideas are still important for the prevention of illness.

Quack or be quacked

Sometimes, in desperation, the settlers turned to quacks. Quacks lied about their healing skills in order to make money. They promised impossible cures. Quacks made a great deal of money from people who wanted to believe in their cures. Quacks claimed to have miracle medicines. They sold tonics made with quinine, alcohol, and water. Some of their cures contained dangerous drugs, such as opium. Quacks advertised their cures in the newspapers. They put up notices in public places, such as the general store. Often it was hard to tell whether a healer was a quack.

The great contributors

The doctors and scientists in this picture have all contributed to modern medicine with their discoveries. In many cases, their discoveries were not taken seriously for a long time. Read about the contributions of these men on the following pages. Match the men and the discoveries with the stories: a) Harvey, b) Leeuwenhoek c) Louis Pasteur, d) Laennec, e) Semmelweis, f) Dr. Lind, g) Lister, h) Jenner, i) the discovery of anesthetics.

Hippocrates, the father of medicine

Hippocrates is called "the father of medicine." He lived in Greece in 460 B.C. He wrote books describing the symptoms of different diseases. He believed that examining the patient thoroughly was the doctor's most important job. Hippocrates realized the importance of cleanliness.

Hippocrates treated medicine as a profession. He expected his medical students to take their work seriously. He made all of his students swear to share their knowledge and to guard the lives of others. His students also vowed not to take advantage of their patients. This meant that they could not discuss the illnesses of their patients without their permission. The doctors had to keep their patients' secrets. This vow taken by the students was called the **Hippocratic Oath.** Doctors today are still expected to follow these rules.

The father of pharmacy

Galen was a Greek doctor born 600 years after Hippocrates. Galen's important contribution to medicine was his ability to prepare and combine medicines into effective remedies. Today approved drugs are sometimes called "galenicals." Galen's name still plays an important part in pharmacy.

The humors of Galen

Galen was certainly well-known in medicine too. Doctors followed his teachings for nearly two thousand years. Unfortunately, many of his ideas about the causes of disease were wrong. Galen's theory of **humors** was based on the ancient Greek belief about the universe. The Greeks thought that the universe was composed of four elements: fire, water, air, and earth. Galen believed that the human body was also composed of four elements, called "humors." The humors were blood, phlegm, yellow bile, and black bile. Galen thought that sickness was caused when the humors were out of balance. His cures were based on correcting the balance of the humors. When the patient seemed to have too much of one kind of humor, the doctor made the patient sweat or bleed to get rid of the excess.

Doctors believed in Galen's theory and used his treatments of bloodletting and blistering for seventeen centuries. The belief in the theory of humors prevented progress in medicine. Doctors were on the wrong track for a long time. Then, Pasteur discovered that many diseases were caused by germs, not body fluids. Galen was also wrong in some of his other teachings!

Holes in Galen's theory

Galen taught that blood flowed back and forth in the body's arteries and veins. He believed that blood ebbed and flowed in the veins in the same way that the ocean tides move to and from the shore. Galen also thought that the walls of the heart contained thick holes. He believed that blood flowed back and forth through these holes and then mixed with the air in the lungs.

Harvey discovers circulatic

For many years, doctors thought Galen was correct. William Harvey disagreed. As a medical student, Harvey dissected the hearts of fish, frogs, and mice. His close examination showed that the heart was made up of four chambers. The four chambers were a right and left ventricle, and a right and left atrium. He also observed that the veins and arteries were formed in such a way that blood could flow only in one direction. Tiny valves stopped blood from going in the opposite direction. With each heartbeat, the blood was pushed through the veins and arteries. Harvey's discovery of the **circulation** of blood was made in the seventeenth century. Many doctors rejected Harvey's beliefs. They continued to believe in Galen's theory until more than one hundred years later.

Leeuwenhoek's tiny pets

Anton van Leeuwenhoek was not a doctor. He owned a drapery business. One of his hobbies was grinding lenses. He used them to look at objects too small to be seen by the naked eye. He put a tiny lens between two sheets of silver or brass. Leeuwenhoek observed bacteria, which he called "animalcules." He loved to shock people by showing them these tiny creatures. He wrote in one of his reports:

"I have had several gentlewomen in my house, who were keen on seeing the little eels in vinegar, but some of them were so disgusted at the spectacle that they vowed they would never use vinegar again. But what if one should tell such people in the future that there are more animals living in the scum on the teeth in a person's mouth, than there are people in a whole kingdom? Especially in those who don't even clean their teeth?"

Leeuwenhoek's work was criticized. It was 200 years before doctors appreciated his contribution to medicine. Many people heard about the "animalcules," but no one connected these bacteria to disease.

Laennec's stethoscope

Theophile Laennec became a doctor in 1804. He was particularly interested in tuberculosis. His mother and many of his friends had died of this disease.

One day, Laennec saw a group of children playing by a pile of hollow beams. One child put his ear to the end of a beam, while another tapped on the opposite end. To Laennec's surprise, the child listening at the end of the beam could hear the tapping clearly. From this, Laennec got an idea. He rolled a piece of paper and used it to listen to someone's heart. He heard the heartbeat more clearly than he had ever heard it before!

Laennec paid a carpenter to make a similar cylinder out of wood. He called this cylinder a **stethoscope**. He used it to study the sounds inside the body. Laennec learned to diagnose heart and lung problems. His stethoscope was a great contribution to medicine. Today, stethoscopes look quite different from Laennec's instrument. They are still one of the doctor's important tools.

Clean advice from Semmelweis

Early doctors did not wash their instruments properly. They also did not do a very good job of washing their hands. Many infections were caused by dirt. A man named Ignaz Semmelweis saved the lives of many people because he insisted that the doctors who worked for him wash their hands carefully.

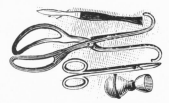

Semmelweis worked in the maternity ward of a hospital in Vienna in 1847. Many mothers who had just given birth died from **puerperal fever**. This "childbed fever," as it was also called, often killed women in maternity wards that were located near the room where **autopsies** were performed. In the autopsy room, doctors examined bodies to find out why people had died. These bodies contained all kinds of bacteria. The doctors who performed autopsies got bacteria all over their hands. When they went to the maternity ward to deliver babies, the bacteria was spread to the women. Women caught infections.

Semmelweis ordered his students to wash their hands in a special solution before going to examine women. Because of this simple act, the lives of many women were saved. There were only a few cases of childbed fever at the hospital where Semmelweis was a doctor.

Even though Semmelweis proved his theory by saving lives, few people believed him. It was hard to imagine that tiny particles, which were invisible, could be transferred from one patient to another on a doctor's hands.

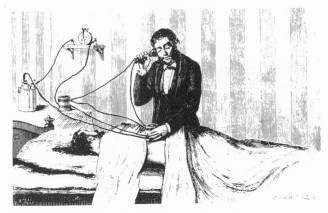

After Jenner developed a vaccination against smallpox, clinics were set up in many towns and cities. People lined up to be vaccinated against the terrible disease which killed many thousands.

Jenner conquers smallpox

The word **smallpox** filled the early settlers with horror. There were few diseases that were so destructive to humans. It was one of the most contagious diseases. It affected all ages, but it was fatal especially to young children and old people. Smallpox was caused by a **virus.** The virus caused little blisters to form on the skin. These **pustules** also formed on the inside of the mouth and throat, where they could swell and prevent breathing. When the victim survived and the pustules began to heal, scabs formed on the skin. When the scabs fell off, scars or **pockmarks** were left.

Sick together, stick together!

There was no **vaccination** against smallpox, but there was a way to prevent a serious case of smallpox. People tried to catch a mild case of the disease from people who were suffering from it. People who survived a case of smallpox did not catch the disease again. To catch the disease, the settlers used arm-to-arm inoculation. This inoculation was difficult to carry out. The smallpox virus was taken from the sores of the people who had been inoculated the previous week. Healthy people cut their skin and rubbed the virus into their wounds. The virus entered their systems. They would get a mild form of smallpox. Sometimes people held smallpox "parties." People were inoculated and suffered together through the fever, shakes, and sores. Young people sometimes met their future husbands and wives at smallpox parties. It seems that people who are sick together, stick together!

Homemade immunity

People who had not been inoculated tried to cat the disease when a mild form of it was making the community sick. Sometimes parents

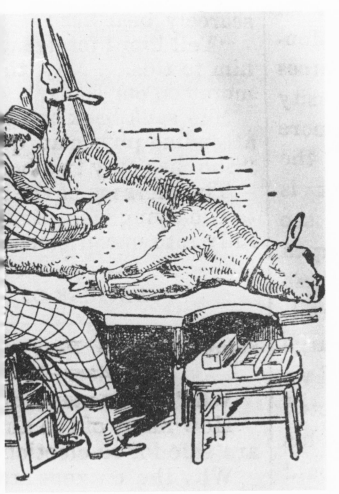

The smallpox vaccine was scraped from the cow-pox pustules on the stomachs of calves. People who were vaccinated got cowpox sores on their arms. However, they did not develop smallpox.

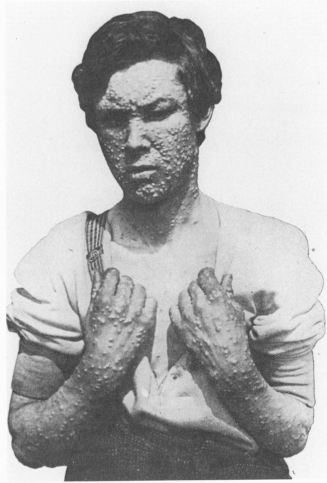

*This unfortunate boy was not vaccinated. He caught smallpox. His body is covered with sores. When he recovers, his face will have small scars called **pockmarks** on it.*

wrapped their children in the clothes of a smallpox victim to cause a mild attack. Other people made a powder from the scabs of a victim's pustules. They inhaled this powder to cause a mild attack. Often this process backfired and a severe attack of smallpox developed.

The cowpox discovery

Dr. Edward Jenner is among the greatest contributors to medicine. He studied in the English countryside during the eighteenth century. He noticed that cows sometimes developed **cowpox.** Pustules formed on their udders. One or two pustules developed on the milkmaid's hands but then went away. Farmers believed that people who had cowpox could not get smallpox. In 1796, Dr. Jenner **inoculated** an eight-year-old boy with cowpox pus. Six weeks later, he inoculated the same boy again, but this time he gave the boy a

dose of smallpox. Dr. Jenner was thrilled when it appeared that the boy was **immune** to smallpox.

Dr. Jenner repeated this experiment on several other people. It was successful every time. He had developed a **vaccination.** Eventually, Dr. Jenner's vaccination was used all over Europe and America. A small amount of vaccine was put on the skin. A few scratches were made in the skin so that the vaccine could enter the body. Immunity to smallpox developed very quickly after vaccination. Today, smallpox is simply "a thing of the past."

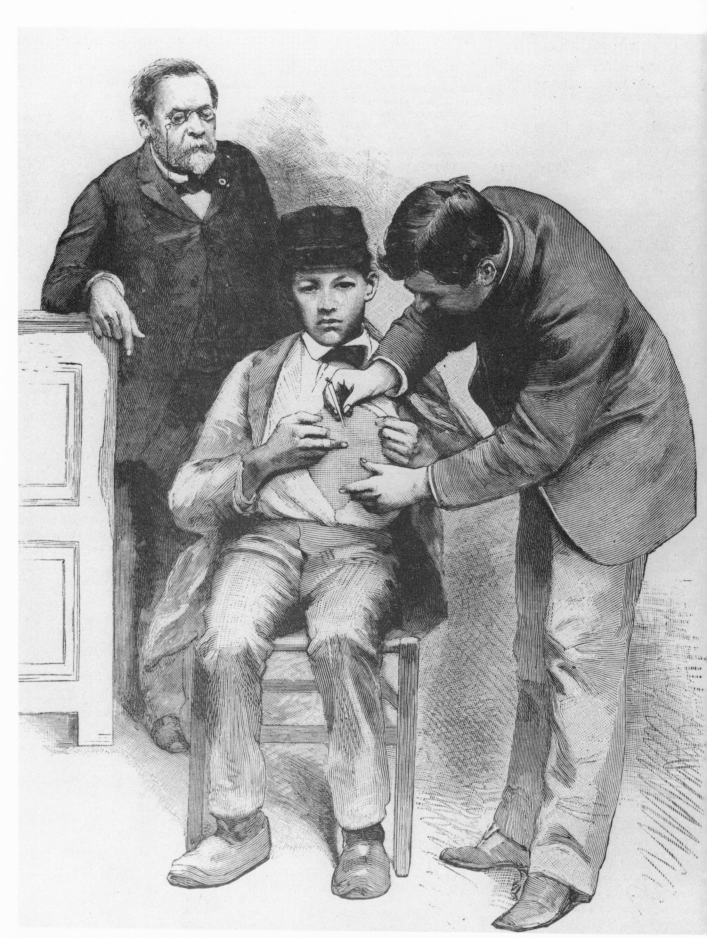

Pasteur looks on as the doctor inoculates this boy. The boy was bitten by a dog with rabies. Before Pasteur's vaccine, a person bitten by a rabid animal died a painful death. The vaccine will save this bo

Pasteur leads the way

Louis Pasteur was the famous French scientist who discovered that germs were a main cause of disease. Pasteur lived in France in an area that was famous for fine wines. He was fascinated by the way the natural sugar in wine grapes changed into alcohol. Big vats of wine began to foam and bubble as the juice turned into wine. The sugar in the juice was changing into alcohol through a process called **fermentation**. Fermentation causes one substance to change into something else.

Pasteur noticed fermentation in other foods. He knew that milk became sour, butter went bad, and meat rotted. He wanted to understand why. Most people thought that fermentation started by itself. Pasteur did not believe that fermentation began spontaneously.

Pasteur collected samples of fermented grape juice, sour milk, rancid butter, and rotten meat. He examined these samples through his powerful microscope. When he looked at the fermented grape juice, Pasteur saw the cells of a fungus called **yeast**. Yeast fungi lived in the air. The fungi caused the sugar to change or decompose into alcohol. Yeast was not found in fresh grape juice. Pasteur then examined samples of spoiled milk, butter, and meat. These samples were full of tiny **bacteria**.

Germs, a cause of disease

Pasteur grew cultures of these rod-shaped bacteria in his laboratory. A culture is a little colony of bacteria which has grown in a special glass dish. Pasteur put these bacteria into fresh milk, butter, meat, and grape juice. The milk went sour, the butter became rancid, and the juice fermented into alcohol.

Pasteur wondered if these bacteria were the same as those that caused diseases in human beings. Pasteur was not the first person to see yeast fungi or bacteria, but he was the first person to realize that these **germs** had something to do with human disease. Foods ferment and spoil all over the world. Pasteur realized that germs, which live in the air, were everywhere. Pasteur continued to experiment with fungi and bacteria. He wrote about his discoveries so that other scientists and doctors could learn about germs.

A cure for rabies

Rabies, or "Mad Dog Disease," as it was sometimes called, was a terrible sickness. Dogs and wild animals often spread the disease. A dog with rabies would froth at the mouth and attack people. A person who was bitten by a rabid dog would become violently ill within 10 to 30 days. Rabies was usually fatal.

Louis Pasteur was determined to find a cure for rabies. He tried to find the cause of rabies by looking for bacteria in the saliva of rabid dogs. Rabies, however, is caused by a virus. A germ is microscopic, but a virus is hundreds of times smaller than a germ. Pasteur's microscope was not powerful enough to make the virus visible.

Pasteur continued to study the disease. He realized that rabies attacked the brain and spinal cord. The observation was important. Pasteur began to collect the spinal cords of rabbits that had died of rabies. He dried the spinal cords and ground them into a fine powder. The powder was made into an anti-toxin. Pasteur experimented with this anti-toxin, but he found that one inoculation was not enough. Rabies was such a powerful disease that a series of shots was needed to prevent it.

On July 6, 1885, a little boy was brought into Pasteur's laboratory. The boy had been badly bitten by a rabid dog. He was inoculated with some of Pasteur's vaccine. Several shots were injected into the boy's stomach. The inoculation worked! News of Pasteur's success spread throughout the world. Within a year, more than 2,000 patients were treated for rabies. They all survived.

Pasteur in his laboratory.

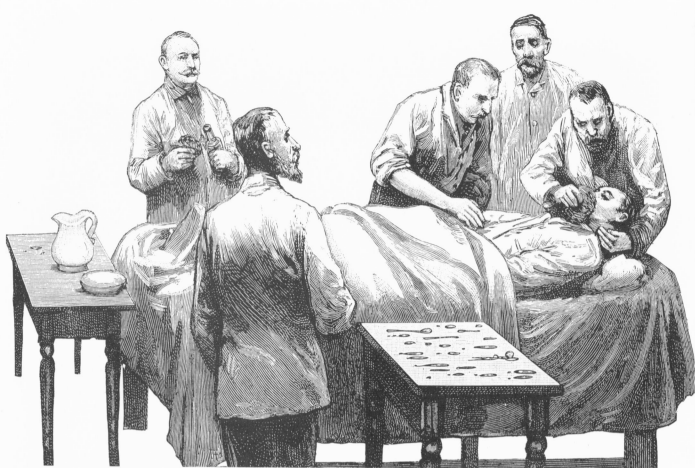

Anesthetics allowed doctors to perform surgery without pain.

Surgery without pain

Have you ever been to the hospital for an operation, or to the dentist to have a cavity filled? When we go to the doctor or the dentist for these treatments, we are given an **anesthetic.** Anesthetics prevent pain. Try to imagine having a tooth filled without something to stop the pain. There were no anesthetics in the days of the settlers.

People tried to find a potion or tonic to kill pain. One of the most popular ways to kill pain was to drink big doses of whiskey or some other liquor. Patients sometimes drank so much that they became unconscious. Other drugs were also used. Many of these drugs, such as morphine, were dangerous. Sponges were soaked with these drugs, and patients sniffed the sponge. Unfortunately, drugged and drunk patients still experienced severe pain during surgery.

Laughing pain away

In 1800, Sir Humphrey Davy discovered a drug that made people laugh instead of suffer. Davy discovered that a gas called **nitrous oxide** stopped pain. It also made people feel happy and laugh out loud. If people breathed much of this gas, they became unconscious. Davy tried this "laughing gas" on himself. He wrote a report that explained his discovery. He suggested that laughing gas might be used in surgical operations to stop pain. Doctors were not willing to accept this new idea.

What a gas!

In 1844, a dentist named Horace Wells used laughing gas on himself. He hoped that it would prevent pain when he had a tooth pulled. The extraction of his tooth was completely painless. Wells tried to explain his findings. Doctors did not accept this new information. Neither doctors nor dentists were convinced that laughing gas was useful until years later. However, the evidence could not be ignored forever. Demonstrations proved that anesthetics worked wonders. **Ether** and **chloroform** were also discovered and used as anesthetics. Doctors could take more time during operations because they did not have to worry about their patients being in pain. Anesthesia was one of America's contributions to world medicine.

Surgery without germs

After surgery, patients often developed fevers and infections. Sometimes hospitals had to be closed because infections spread to all the patients. Doctors could not figure out why these infections occurred. They did not know that they themselves were to blame! Doctors and medical students did not know about germs. They did not know that it was important to wash their hands before examining patients. Doctors wore their street clothes into the operating and examination rooms. They carried germs on their clothes as well as on their hands.

Lister learns from Pasteur

A Scottish doctor named Joseph Lister was worried about surgical infection. Lister was interested in Louis Pasteur's germ research. Lister also thought that the same bacteria that made wine ferment and meat rot might be responsible for surgical infection. Pasteur's experiments demonstrated that germs were killed by heat and by special chemicals called **antiseptics.** This knowledge filled Lister with the hope that surgical infections could be stopped.

Saving a leg

One day, a little boy was brought to Dr. Lister's office. He had a compound fracture. His bone was so badly broken that it stuck out of a gash in his skin. At that time, most surgeons amputated in cases of compound fracture. Infections almost always set in because compound fractures were open wounds. Unfortunately, many patients died when the limbs were amputated.

Dr. Lister decided not to amputate. Instead, he carefully cleaned the wound and set the bone straight again. The first antiseptic Lister used was **carbolic acid.** He covered the wound with a large bandage which had been soaked in it. With this sterilized bandage, all the germs on the boy's wound were killed and new germs could not infect it. To the astonishment of Lister's colleagues, the boy's leg healed without becoming infected.

Spraying germs away

Lister wanted to improve hospital surgery by eliminating infections. He devised a machine which spread a fine spray of carbolic acid around the operating room. The spray killed

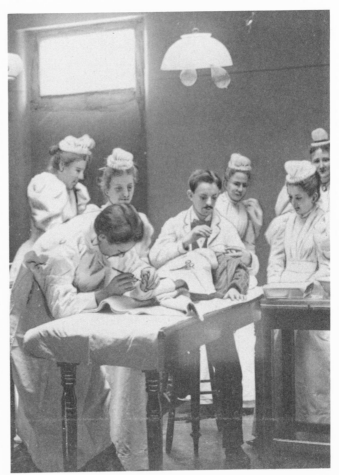

The doctors and nurses in this old photograph are wearing hospital gowns instead of suits. However, they are not wearing masks, caps, or gloves.

the germs. After Lister began practicing **antisepsis** or the killing of germs, wounds no longer became **septic** or infected. Few people died from infection in the hospital surgery wards.

Keeping germs out

Lister made an enormous contribution to medicine. His method of killing germs during an operation saved many lives. It opened many doors for new and difficult operations. Doctors also realized that it made more sense to keep germs out of the operating room in the first place. Germs were killed on surgical instruments and dressings before an operation, not during one. Doctors and nurses started wearing sterilized surgical gowns, masks, hair caps, and rubber gloves, so that their germs could not come into contact with open wounds during surgery. Lister's method of killing germs was called antisepsis. "Anti" is a prefix which can mean "working against." Antisepsis means "working against germs." Doctors could perform germ-free operations. The new kind of operating was called "asepsis." This word means "without germs."

In the days of the settlers, everyone in the community took turns nursing the sick. The minister has dropped in to read a Bible story to Katie. She has been ill for two weeks. Her brother and sisters keep her company. They also enjoy listening to the story.

Most of the settlers preferred to be nursed at home. The early hospitals were terrible. Rats scampered all over the floor and the beds. Often the patients did not receive proper care. Sometimes, patients became sicker after they went into the hospital.

Caring for the sick

Today many people choose nursing as a career. In the early days nursing was not considered a profession. Sick people were nursed at home by members of their family. People in the community also helped. When settlers were ill, their friends brought food over. Neighbors spent time with sick friends, cheering them up or reading to them. The village school-masters visited their students and others in the community who were ill. The minister called on people who were sick and read them verses from the Bible. Wealthy people sometimes hired women to look after bedridden family members. In the early days it was better for people to be nursed at home. Those who went into the hospital often did not return.

Horrible hospitals

Hospitals were dirty. Rats were everywhere. Rats carried diseases. Hospitals were over-crowded. Hospital nursing was done by women who were too old and weak to do anything else. They received little or no pay. People who could not get jobs anywhere else also did nursing. Sometimes these people stole from the hospital patients. In some hospitals, patients who were not gravely ill looked after the other patients. Often these patients caught the diseases of the people they nursed. Nursing was not thought to be a job for well-trained people.

The Lady of the Lamp

Nursing was just as terrible in Europe as it was here. It took someone special to realize the importance of nursing sick people. Florence Nightingale was that person. Nightingale was a wealthy English woman who was born in Italy. She believed that nursing should be a responsible profession. She felt health care should be available to everyone who needed it. During the Crimean War, she led a team of nurses to the battlefront to care for wounded soldiers. Many of the wounded were suffering from cholera. Nightingale immediately opened five kitchens and a laundry to feed the soldiers properly and keep them in clean clothes. Under her direction, many lives were saved. Florence Nightingale was known as "the Lady of the Lamp." Night and day, she comforted the sick soldiers. When a wounded soldier needed water or medicine at night, Florence was there, shining her lamp on him, to find out how she could ease his suffering.

In 1860 Florence opened the Nightingale Training School for Nurses. She wanted to teach people how to nurse the sick properly. After one year, the students were graduated as nurses. They were called **probationers.** Nightingale expected her students to have high moral values. If students were caught being untruthful even in a small matter, they were dismissed.

Although Nightingale was from a wealthy family, she wished to offer the opportunity of nursing to girls from humble homes. Two types of students were admitted to her school. Girls from wealthy families had to pay an enrollment fee. Students from poor families did not have to pay tuition. Their fee was paid by the Nightingale Fund.

The school received many applications for admission. In its first few years, there were between 1,000 and 2,000 applications for 15 to 30 positions. Nurses worked 11 to 12 hours a day. They were expected to have cheerful personalities. They had to be strong enough to face pain and death. Many young women wanted to become nurses in order to get away from home. Many men applied to become nurses as well.

Graduates from the Nightingale School were not always welcomed in hospitals. Older doctors were afraid that trained nurses would question their authority. Some doctors did not like working with women who came from a higher social class. Nevertheless, improvements in nursing and hospital care quickly spread all over the world. New standards were set in health care. The spirit of Florence Nightingale still lives on in our hospitals today.

Doctors started to specialize. A doctor became an expert in one area of medicine and did not treat patients for all ailments. This doctor is an **ophthalmologist.** *He treats eye diseases.*

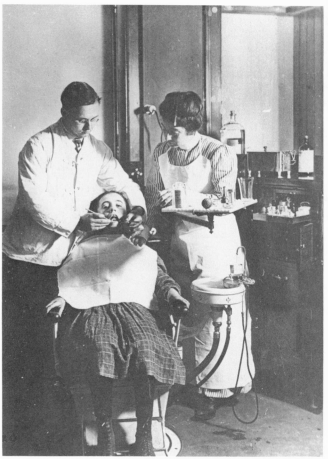

Dentists also formed associations. They did not simply pull teeth. They checked people's teeth and taught them how to prevent cavities.

Raising medical standards

Many of the settlers who called themselves doctors were trained by other doctors. They did not study medicine in school. A few doctors were trained in European medical schools, but most of them learned by doing. These apprentice doctors started their own practices when their teachers felt they were ready. The length of training differed from one doctor to the next. Apothecaries, dentists, and homeopaths had their own special skills, but some of them also called themselves doctors. The special skill of apothecaries was mixing medicines, but they also treated sick people. Today, apothecaries cannot give medicines to patients. Doctors must first give the prescriptions for drugs.

Crackdown on quacks

Medicine is a difficult subject for people to understand. The settlers simply had to trust that their doctors knew their business. Unfortunately, there were many quacks who fooled people. Quacks promised quick cures, and people believed them. Doctors fought back against the quacks, who gave medicine a bad name. Doctors formed **associations** throughout the country. Doctors decided that people who called themselves doctors had to have licences before they could practice. They could only be **certified** as doctors after they had passed strict examinations. Doctors could no longer be apothecaries and dentists. Dentists could not be doctors. Each profession was separate and specialized. Doctors decided they all should charge the same fees for their services. These fees were set by the new medical associations. Many quacks were put out of business.

People began to believe that doctors were well trained. They trusted certified doctors. More people went to doctors for help, and more people became good doctors. Medical schools opened in the big cities. Doctors discovered new information about the causes and cures of disease. Medicine became a highly respected profession.

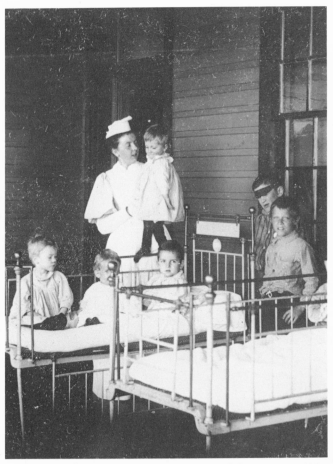

Hospitals for sick children opened in many cities. Children were treated with loving care. Special treatments were developed to help children.

The first female doctors were not accepted by most of the patients and other doctors. They soon proved that they were as capable as men.

Women are not welcome

Medicine was a profession for men. Even though women were the ones who collected the herbs for the family and did the home "doctoring," they were not allowed into the medical profession. Many people believed that a woman's brain was simply too small to learn the large amount of information that a doctor had to know. Women could only become nurses and **midwives**. Midwives were women who delivered babies.

In the nineteenth century, it was hard for women to enter medical school. Even when they were accepted and became doctors, patients would not go to them. Few people trusted the skills of women doctors.

One woman disguised herself as a man in order to get a medical education. Doctor James Barry dressed as a man all her life so that she could practice as a doctor. She was such an excellent physician that she

became chief surgeon in the army. People did not disover that she was a woman until after her death in 1865. She kept her secret until she died. In the last one hundred years, more and more women have pursued careers in medicine. Today, both men and women doctors enjoy the same professional status. Women doctors no longer have to hide the fact that they are women. Many people prefer to have women as their doctors.

New organizations, such as the Red Cross, helped many sick people.

59

Miracles of modern medicine

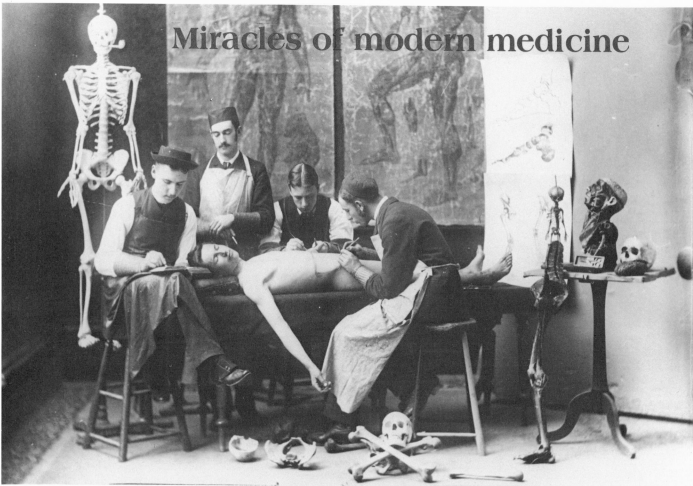

These early medical students have posed for this picture. As more medical colleges opened, many people left their bodies to science so that doctors could study their bodies and learn more about disease. The students are pretending that they are examining a body. Their friend is playing dead. The students try to shock people by displaying skulls and skeletons in the photograph.

*Doctors learned to give **blood transfusions.** The early transfusions often failed because doctors did not know people had different blood types.*

Vaccinations against smallpox gave children a better chance for survival. Doctors came to schools to make sure that all children were given vaccinations.

60

The discovery of x-ray photographs was an important step in learning about disease and the human body. Tuberculosis could be spotted in its early stages. Doctors were also able to see broken bones and tumors inside the body. The early x-ray machines, however, made people ill because of high levels of radiation.

These children all have eye problems. Thanks to advances in medicine, they were helped by operations and special glasses.

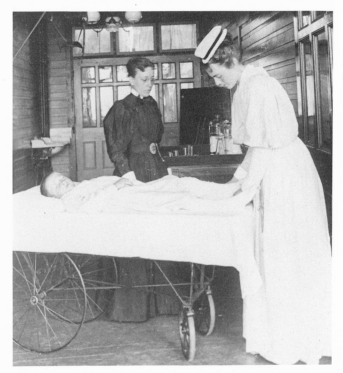

New operations helped to correct birth defects. Arms and legs could be set in casts. Afterward, they were as good as new.

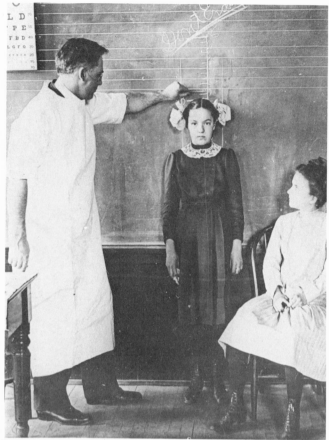

In later years, people discovered the basics of good health. Regular checkups were important. Early diagnosis of diseases made cures simpler.

The settlers learned that keeping clean was important to health. People began to bathe and to clean their teeth more often.

Back to basics

After Pasteur discovered the germ, people realized that many of their habits had been making them sick. The settlers began to bathe more often and to brush their teeth regularly. People also learned more about nutrition. They ate a variety of fresh foods straight from their gardens. They drank pasteurized milk.

As life became more complicated, people started to get sloppy about their health. Fast foods replaced fresh fruit and vegetables. Hot dogs and hamburgers became staple foods! Sugar, salt, and chemical preservatives were added to canned and frozen foods. People found it easier to gulp down quick meals than to plan healthy menus. They figured that the extra vitamins they took could make up for the nutrients that were missing in their food. Many people became overweight and out of shape.

In recent years, there has been a new effort toward better health. People are realizing that a good diet and regular exercise are

basic to staying healthy. People have begun to eat fresh fruit and vegetables instead of canned and frozen foods. People jog, swim, and play sports. The settlers' belief that "an ounce of prevention is worth a pound of cure" is shared by many people today.

Glossary

ague a name for a fever and periods of chills and sweating

ailment an illness which may last for a long time

anesthetic a drug that deadens pain and causes unconsciousness

antidote anything that removes the effects of a disease or poison

antiseptic able to destroy or prevent growth of harmful bacteria

antitoxin a substance that can protect against some diseases

apothecary a druggist or pharmacist; also, an early term for a drug store

apprenticeship the fixed amount of time a person must spend working for another person in order to learn a trade or business

artery one of the tubes that carry blood away from the heart to all parts of the body

arthritis a swelling and feeling of pain in joints of the body

bacillus (pl. bacilli) a bacterium shaped like a rod or cylinder

bacterium (pl. bacteria) a tiny plant that can only be seen with a microscope; some bacteria cause diseases

blood transfusion the putting of blood into a person's body

blood vessels the tubes in the body through which blood travels

cauterize to burn living tissue with a hot iron, in order to prevent infection

cell the smallest part of any living animal or plant

chemotherapy the use of chemical substances to treat diseases

contagious easily spread from person to person

croup a children's throat disease marked by difficult breathing and a high-pitched cough

culture the growth of bacteria or viruses in a special preparation; it is used for scientific study

diagnosis recognizing a disease by its symptoms

diarrhea a condition in which the bowels move too loosely

disability something that makes a person less able

dislocate to put a bone out of joint

distillation the process of heating a liquid until it evaporates, and then cooling it until it becomes a liquid again

distillery a place where alcoholic liquors are made by distillation

dysentery a disease of the intestines causing diarrhea and pain

epidemic the sudden spread of disease among many people

ether a colorless liquid used to make people unconscious for operations

fatal causing death

fermentation a process by which the sugar in a liquid slowly turns into alcohol and a gas

fever a body temperature higher than normal

fracture a break or crack, as in a bone

fungus (pl. fungi) one of a large group of plants that have no flowers, no leaves, and no green coloring; yeast is a fungus

germ a very tiny animal or plant that can cause disease

gruel a thin, liquid food made by boiling cereal in water or milk

hemorrhage a flow of blood, usually heavy and from a blood vessel

hygiene the science of health; also, healthful rules and practices

immigrant a person who moves into one country from another

immune protected against a disease

infection a disease caused by germs or viruses

infectious spread by infection

inflammation a diseased condition of some part of the body, shown by heat, redness, swelling, and pain

influenza the flu; a disease that causes fever, coughing, and pains in the chest and muscles

inoculate to put a special form of the germs of a disease into a person's or an animal's body, to prevent or cure that disease

intern a recent graduate of medical school who helps to treat patients in a hospital

intestines two coiled tubes that extend from the stomach and help us to digest food

joint a point in a person's body where parts or bones are joined in a way that allow them to move

laryngitis an inflammation of the voice box (the larynx), often marked by a hoarse voice

liniment a liquid rubbed on the skin to ease pain or stiffness

malady a disease, sickness, or illness

membrane a thin layer of tissue that covers or lines certain parts of people, animals, and plants

miasma a heavy vapor rising from the earth, once thought to cause disease

mucus a thick, slimy liquid that protects the insides of the throat, the mouth, and other body parts

nineteenth century the years 1801 to 1900

nutrient food; something that provides us with what is needed to grow and develop

nutrition the use of food to help us grow and develop

ointment a thick, oily substance used as medicine for the skin

ophthalmologist a doctor who treats diseases of the eyes

pap soft food for babies or sick people

parasite an animal or plant that lives in or on another and gets its food from the other

pasteurization to heat milk or other liquids in order to destroy bacteria

phial, vial a small bottle for liquids

pneumonia a serious disease of the lungs

poliomyelitis a contagious disease that can cause paralysis, damaged muscles, and sometimes death; the disease affects mainly children; today there is a vaccine to prevent it

poultice a moist, hot mass of flour or mustard, applied to a sore part of the body

preservative something that is added to foods to keep them from spoiling

pulse the beating of the arteries as the heart pumps blood

pustule a small swelling of the skin, containing pus

quack someone who pretends to have great knowledge, usually about medicine

quarantine to separate from others to prevent the spread of an infectious disease

quinine a bitter, colorless drug used to treat malaria and other diseases

radiation waves or particles used in x-ray photographs; too much radiation can harm the skin and body tissues

saliva the tasteless, colorless liquid produced in the mouth

sanitarium a place for the care and treatment of patients who have certain diseases, such as tuberculosis

scarlet fever a contagious disease that is marked by a bright red rash, a high fever, and a sore throat

septic causing infection

spasm a sudden, unexpected drawing together of a muscle

sterilize to free from harmful bacteria or germs

superstition a belief that one action will cause a second action not related to it; believing 13 to be an unlucky number is a common superstition

teething the growing or developing of teeth

tendon a tough band of tissue that connects a muscle to a bone

tissue in an animal or a plant, a group of cells that make up a certain part of the body or the plant

toxin a poison produced in a person's or an animal's body by certain bacteria

tuberculosis an infectious disease that can affect any part of the body, especially the lungs and joints

typhoid fever a fever caused by bacteria in bad water and food; it causes reddish spots on the skin and inflammation of the intestines

typhus a disease caused by germs carried by fleas or lice; it causes a headache, high fever, and a spotted rash

uric acid a chemical produced in man and other animals

vaccination giving a vaccine to prevent certain diseases

vaccine weak or dead disease germs, prepared and injected as a protection against that disease

vacuum an area where air pressure is reduced; a vacuum can create suction

vein the vessels that carry blood back to the heart

vessel see blood vessel

virus a tiny form of living matter, smaller than bacteria; viruses cause many diseases

x ray a photograph taken with x rays or particles of energy

yeast a tiny plant that breaks down sugar to produce alcohol

Index

Acknowledgements

Library of Congress, Dover Archives, Colonial Williamsburg, Century Village, Lang, Upper Canada Village, Black Creek Pioneer Village, Metropolitan Toronto Library, Colborne Lodge, Toronto Historical Board, Gibson House, City of Toronto Archives, Bibliotheque Nationa du Quebec, Harper's Weekly, Canadian Illustrated News, Public Archives of Canada, Notman Photographic Archives, Little Wide Awake, Frank Leslie's Illustrated Magazine, the Osborne Collection of Early Children's Books, Toronto Public Library, the Buffalo and Erie Coun Public Library Rare Book Department, Jamestown, Chatterbox, McCord Museum, Harper's Round Table Magazine, Museum of the Histo of Medicine, U of T Faculty of Pharmacy, John P. Roberts Library.

1415 LB Printed in the U.S.A. 98